I'm a Leader, Now What?

A HANDBOOK FOR THE NEW LEADER

Wendy Norfleet, Ph.D.

Published by:

11250 Old St. Augustine Rd
Suite 15-173
Jacksonville, FL 32257
NorfleetSolutions.com

ISBN: 978-1-7356304-1-0

Library of Congress Control Number: 2020916284

First Edition
Printed in the United States of America

Cover Designed by Jeane Sumner, Website HQ

Disclaimer

This book is designed to provide readers with information and guidance and supplements coaching, mentoring, and professional development training.

DEDICATION

To all the aspiring and new leaders.

I'm a Leader, Now What?
You've been given a role to lead,
A change to inspire and succeed,
To guide your team towards the light,
And help them shine with all their might.

It's a daunting task to take on,
But with courage and heart, you'll be strong,
For leadership is not just a title,
It's a way of life that's vital.

You'll face challenges along the way,
But never forget to seize the day,
To listen and encourage your team,
And help them achieve their dream.

So, take the reins and lead with pride,
With heart and mind open wide,
For you have been given a chance to shine,
And make a difference, one step at a time.

Wendy Norfleet, PhD

CONTENTS

ACKNOWLEDGMENTS

Being a leader is not easy. As I think back, I am sure my leadership skills started within my family. I thank my family and friends for helping shape me into the person I am.

I thank all my previous leaders, the good and the bad, for teaching me life lessons.

Lastly, I thank God for continually watching over me and blessing me.

INTRODUCTION

"Ambition is the first step to success. The second step is action."

Unknown

Okay, you set your eyes on a leadership role, worked hard, and you've now arrived at your destination. You are the leader. Now what? Don't just stand there with a deer in the headlights. Look, it's time to show what you've got! I realize that it is not always that easy. While most companies do an excellent job of providing specific skills training, there is an overall lack of training for new leaders. Added to that, you may now lead those once your peers. Rest assured, help is on the way.

One of my first clients was a new leader who was

also new to the organization – let's call her Margaret. Like any good candidate, she researched the company, understanding its mission, values, and goals. She could not wait to get started. Finally, her first day arrived. She spent half of it onboarding and the other half getting settled and saying hello to those who reported to her. The following day, she had her first department meeting. She planned for this meeting all night, jotting down her ideas on her department vision and how she wanted things to run. So far, so good. When she arrived the next day, after providing a more detailed self-introduction, she shared her ideas and the actions she wanted to take. Was this the best way to officially meet her staff?

The scenario above is just food for thought before you delve into this book's exciting content. By the time you have reached the end, you will have already thought of an answer to the question posed above, with greater insights into what will make you a great leader. As you read, you will get an in-depth look at actual situations and best practices for a variety of topics that include:

- Setting Expectations Early

- Being a Visible Leader
- Holding Amazing Meetings
- Building Relationships
- Managing Difficult Team Members

So, I implore you to read with the goal in mind that you will be asked profound questions and will need to do some deep reflection on your preconceived notion of who a leader is. Then you have to consider what qualities you already possess and then what other characteristics you need to display in order to make your leadership role most effective to not only benefit the productivity and morale of those you lead but also to continue to build that confidence and pride as a means of personal development

CHAPTER 1: SET EXPECTATIONS EARLY

"Nobody rises to low expectations.:"

Calvin Lloyd

As a new leader, it is essential to set expectations early to establish a clear direction for your team and avoid misunderstandings or miscommunications that can lead to conflict or confusion. Think of captaining a ship. If the crew members do not know where you are headed and have no idea of the route and tasks needed to be completed so that you can arrive at the destination safely, how likely will that trip be successful? Also, setting expectations requires careful planning and communication and a willingness to listen to feedback and adjust as needed.

Taking on a leadership position, especially as a budding leader, can be challenging and exciting at the same time. Your main desire is to establish the vision and direction for your team or department. Actions that will help you set these expectations as a new leader include:

1. **Define the Scope of Your Role**

Before setting expectations for your team or department, it is vital to understand the scope of your role and the responsibilities that come with it. This includes understanding your team's goals, the expectations of your senior leaders and team members, and any limitations or constraints that may affect your ability to lead effectively. By clarifying your role, you can set realistic and achievable expectations. Was it clear in the scenario provided in the Introduction that this was what Margaret did? How can one understand the scope of one's role as a leader without any thoughtful conversation about such with those you are about to lead?

2. **Identify Key Stakeholders**

So, as a new leader, it is crucial to identify and build relationships with key stakeholders who can help support and guide you as you navigate your new role. These stakeholders may include your direct reports, peers, mentors, and senior leaders in your organization. By understanding their perspectives and expectations, you can better align your expectations with those of your team and the organization.

3. Clearly Communicate Expectations

Therefore, once you clearly understand your role and those of your key stakeholders, it's time to clearly communicate your expectations to your team. This includes setting clear goals and objectives, outlining performance expectations, and establishing guidelines for communication and collaboration. It is essential to communicate these expectations in a way that is easy to understand and allows for feedback and questions.

4. Listen to Feedback and Adjust as Needed

As you communicate your expectations, it is essential to listen to feedback from your team and be willing to adjust your expectations as needed. This may include revising goals or performance expectations based on input or altering your communication and collaboration guidelines to suit the needs of your team better. You can build a culture of trust and collaboration with your team by being open to feedback and willing to adjust your expectations.

5. Lead by Example

For any leader, especially a new leader, it's crucial to lead by example and model the behaviors and expectations that you want to see in your team. This includes demonstrating strong communication skills, being responsive to feedback, and being willing to collaborate and work together towards common goals. Leading by example can set the tone for your team and create a culture of accountability and excellence.

6. Ongoing Feedback and Coaching

By now, we would have recognized that Margaret missed a few steps, but we know that she did indeed set goals and expectations for the team. However, setting expectations is an ongoing process, and providing constant feedback and coaching to your team as they work towards achieving their goals is vital. Consider the following activities that foster continued feedback and coaching: providing regular feedback on performance, coaching team members on areas for improvement, and recognizing and rewarding successes. By providing ongoing feedback and coaching, you can help your team stay focused and motivated as they work towards achieving their goals. And a little incentive can't hurt in sweetening the deal.

Why do you think the Employee of the Month accolade is so effective in many companies?

7. Continuously Evaluate and Adjust

Leaders must continuously evaluate and adjust expectations as needed. Revision of goals or performance expectations based on changing circumstances or adjusting communication and collaboration guidelines to meet the needs of your team better is the actions of a good leader and ensures that your team stays on the path to achieving their goals.

Setting expectations early as a new leader is essential in establishing a clear direction for your team and building a culture of accountability and excellence. But note that by defining the scope of your role and identifying key stakeholders, you will be better able to communicate your expectations clearly and set the tone of listening to feedback and adjusting as needed. You should lead by example, provide ongoing feedback and coaching, and continuously evaluate and adjust. With all these steps, you are setting yourself and your team up for success and closer to achieving your goals as a leader.

CHAPTER 2: DEVELOP A LEADERSHIP ATTITUDE

"Leadership is practiced not so much in words as in attitude and actions."

Harold S. Geneen

Leadership is not just a position or title; it's also an attitude. We've all met people that we can point to and say, "Wow, they have a great leadership attitude!" A leadership attitude embodies confidence, vision, and the ability to inspire and motivate others toward a common goal. Developing a leadership attitude takes time and effort, but with the right mindset and approach, anyone can cultivate the qualities and characteristics of a great leader.

1. **Start with Self-Awareness**

The first step in developing a leadership attitude is to have self-awareness. This means understanding your strengths, weaknesses, values, and personality traits. By understanding yourself better, you can identify areas for improvement and focus on developing the qualities that will help you become a better leader. Here is where you can do your own self-assessment. Consider the job description: Is there a task that you cannot confidently execute? What resources do you need to gather or skills you need to further develop so that you can perform this task well?

But it is not only about the areas you need to improve. You already have some great qualities, which made you a great match for the role in the first place. What are you good at? Someone who is great at presentations would use this skill set to their advantage. Instead of written monthly reports, you may accompany such with great presentations that will not only provide the information in a more exciting way but bring about greater clarity and motivate staff to remain focused on the goals of the team.

2. Set Goals

Once you better understand yourself, setting

goals for your leadership development is essential. These goals should be specific, measurable, achievable, relevant, and time-bound (SMART). For example, you might create a plan to improve your communication skills by taking a public speaking course or to improve your decision-making skills by seeking opportunities to make tough decisions. But do not set yourself up for failure. Taking on too much at once is not recommended. Take small steps towards improvement, as this takes time. And that is why you need to ensure that your goals are truly SMART.

3. Develop Your Emotional Intelligence

This is key when at the helm of the ship. Emotional intelligence is the ability to understand and manage your own emotions, as well as the feelings of others. This skill is critical for leaders, allowing them to communicate effectively, build strong relationships, and navigate difficult situations. To develop your emotional intelligence, focus on listening actively, being empathetic, and developing self-awareness.

Being a ruthless leader who pushes staff aggressively to complete tasks does allow the team to achieve goals, but at what end? When staff eventually feel underappreciated and disrespected, how long will this approach be effective? Understanding your team and what motivates them is also an indicator of your emotional intelligence as a leader.

4. Learn from Mentors and Role Models

One of the best ways to develop a leadership attitude is to learn from others who have already succeeded as leaders. Seek mentors and role models who can provide guidance, advice, and support as you work to develop your leadership skills. Reading this book written by someone who has vast experience as an effective leader is a great start. But you can also look for people who embody the qualities you want to build or improve and ask for their insights and perspectives. Observe their behavior and seek to emulate those qualities that you believe make them great leaders. Or have discussions with them and seek their input on matters. They have a wealth of knowledge and experiences to share.

5. Practice Positive Thinking

Smile for a while, and then give your face a rest. Being a leader doesn't mean that you are always happy, but you have to maintain a positive attitude despite harsh circumstances. A positive mindset is essential for developing a leadership attitude. Positive thinking can help you stay motivated, overcome challenges, and inspire others to do their best. To cultivate a positive mindset, focus on your strengths, visualize success, and surround yourself with supportive people.

6. Take Action

But all the advice given so far in this book is null and void if you do not implement them. Take action toward your leadership goals! This means stepping outside your comfort zone, taking risks, and putting yourself in positions where you can practice and develop your leadership skills. Look for opportunities to lead within your organization or personal life and be willing to take on challenges and responsibilities.

As mentioned before, developing a leadership attitude is something that takes time to happen. It takes time, effort, and a willingness to learn and grow. By focusing on self-awareness, setting goals, developing emotional intelligence, learning from mentors and role models, practicing positive thinking, and taking action, you can cultivate the qualities and characteristics of a great leader. With persistence and dedication, you can become the kind of leader who inspires others to achieve their full potential.

CHAPTER 3: EMBODY THE CHARACTERISTICS OF A GOOD LEADER

"Overall, the challenge of leadership is both moral and one of developing the characteristics that make us respected by one another"

Louis Farrakhan

Most have encountered a memorable leader, whether bad or good. Believe it or not, you can learn life lessons from both. As much as one knows the leadership qualities you wish to harness, you also know the ones that you do not want. The qualities of a bad leader can be quickly identified based on the negative experiences of being led by this person. Note that "Employees do not leave good jobs; they leave bad leaders."

Bad leaders make common mistakes that cause dedicated, productive staff to leave. These mistakes include:

- Being unavailable
- Micromanaging
- Irresponsible actions
- Lack of unaccountability
- Disrespect
- Emotional disconnection
- Exuding toxicity in the workplace

A good leader avoids these mistakes and strives to be effective each day. As a new leader, you should treat your team fairly to earn their respect. You want to become a leader who motivates staff and inspires your team to go the extra mile for you.

A good leader is concerned, helpful, and exudes a sense of purpose. It is said that a good leader is easy to recognize as they embody the following characteristics:

- **Available** - They understand that even the best team member may have questions or need direction.

- **Trust the team** – A good leader trusts their team members' abilities and does not micromanage.
- **Responsible** – Effective leaders make rational decisions that benefit the entire team. They can be counted on to do what needs to be done.
- **Take charge** – Leaders do not wait for others; they take control. They also know that they are accountable for their actions and do not shift the blame on others on the team.
- **Value the time of others** – A good leader recognizes that time is valuable and does not add useless tasks or meetings.
- **Respect all employees** – All employees want to feel valued. Value can be provided through remembering information such as the team member's name, information about their family, birthdays, and work anniversaries.
- **Provide feedback** – Feedback and recognition are necessary. All team members need feedback or constructive advice for improvement. Recognizing a job well done is essential for retention. Show team members that you appreciate their hard work.

- **Cultivating a team attitude** - Create an environment where team members can come to you when they need support or have new ideas. They should know that even though you are the leader, their contributions are invaluable.

Building a Team

All the qualities discussed above will let you steer that dream team toward success. Acknowledging that everyone within your team brings different skills and abilities, as a good leader, you must create an environment where everyone is working together. However, this does not mean that there will not be occasional conflict. You must understand that every team member has a part to play and take the right steps to build a harmonious team.

I remember taking on a new leadership position in which I oversaw multiple teams of about 75 individuals. As you can imagine, there were a lot of personalities and opinions to deal with. By practicing the characteristics of a good leader, I was able to build trust within the team and create productive, cohesive teams that were high-performing. Was it easy? No, but with hard work, it was achievable.

One of the things I emphasized with my teams was to think of us like a family. We each had unique skills and individual personalities. While I encouraged healthy discussion and debate among ourselves, we were to be on our "company behavior" when we were out in front of others. It was a little rough getting this concept adopted, but after a time, I noticed the team members started reminding each other that we did not discuss family conflicts in front of others.

One aspect of a leader that is often overlooked is that the leader should be part of the team. I know everyone does not agree with me, but I have seen it to be true over and over again. Additionally, it can have a tremendously positive impact on the morale and productivity of your team. You are leading the team, but every member is valuable, so if the team fails, all members, including the leader, fail.

While working for a large, global organization, when starting my engineering career, there were two general managers, the equivalent of vice presidents. One managed the manufacturing departments, and the other, the one I worked under, was in charge of engineering. There came a time when everyone had to work Saturdays for extended months due to a major project deadline. The manufacturing general manager told his staff they had to be present, but he left early on Fridays and was not seen again until Monday morning. My general manager came in every Saturday and openly stated that while he did not have the programming skills of his team, he most certainly could make coffee, make copies, and order lunch. Each Saturday, he stayed the entire time with us. Now which general manager do you think was considered part of the team?

Above all else, a good leader cares. That's really what it boils down to. Building that strong team means that they know you have their best interest at heart. This is where emotional intelligence, which was discussed before, truly comes into play. Lead with heart - build genuine relationships and trust amongst your team, which is only possible with you leading the way to do so.

CHAPTER 4: MEETING YOUR NEW TEAM

"Coming together is a beginning; keeping together is progress; working together is success."

Henry Ford

By now, you have an idea of where Margaret went wrong when she met her team for the first time. Too often, new leaders want to assert authority immediately without getting to know their new team. Remember that the better you get to know your team, their roles, and capabilities, the stronger the relationship foundation.

For many, meeting your new team for the first time can cause anxiety. While you want to demonstrate your leadership, you also want to be part of the team and ensure a successful first encounter. If you come on as overbearing or dictatorial, you alienate them. However, you can also fail by being too much of a part of the team and allowing them total control. During this initial introductory meeting, strive for a tone that will enable you to use this opportunity to begin learning and understanding your team.

To be better prepared for this initial meeting, there are a few things that you can do.

- **Do Your Research**
  With the many tools available, you can do both formal and informal research on those you will be leading. Initial and valuable insight into your team will be gained as a result of this research. Social media is at your fingertips, and additionally, there may be the company's intranet and official documents, such as employee records, including employee performance reviews, available to obtain information.

  This is not so as to dig up their personal information to be used as an arsenal in the future. With emotional intelligence applied, you will be learning a little about their culture, and any customs you observe can be beneficial when working with culturally diverse teams. You would hate to make a grievous misstep during your first encounter with your team.

- **Prepare for Your First Team Encounter**
  If meeting in person, selecting a neutral location, such as a conference room or an offsite restaurant, is better than convening the initial meeting in your office. Strive for a comfortable, informal first meeting to reduce stress and promote communication. Well-thought-out icebreakers and brainstorming activities are ways in which to start building rapport with your team. This is a way to set the tone of open communication and make them feel as if their input is valued.

  If meeting virtually, ensure that everything works before the meeting. This may entail setting up a practice session to confirm that you can perform all necessary activities during the meeting. Remember to check your background to ensure it is appropriate. You can also include virtual icebreakers and brainstorming activities.

- **Ease into the Meeting**
  Starting your first team meeting with some small talk that begins building relationships. You want to create a positive meeting environment. This is where icebreakers are very useful. You can start by sharing information about yourself. It does not have to be too personal, but sharing will help your team get to know you and encourage them to talk about themselves. However, do not force team members to share, as it takes some longer to open up.

  There are numerous icebreaker activities that are not too intrusive but can build rapport. For example, the activity of two truths and one lie. In this game, persons share three statements, two will be the truth, and one will be a lie. Team members will be asked to guess which of the three statements is a lie. When you start this as a new leader, your team will get to know you better, as well as set the tone for others to share.

- **Set the Example**
  Be aware that the actions and tone you take at this initial meeting may be associated with the way you will lead. Create a pleasant, respectful atmosphere in which team members feel valued. Therefore, choose activities that will showcase your leadership qualities.

- **Keep It Brief**
  While meeting your team as soon as possible is essential, keep your initial meeting brief and informal. After providing your initial comments, let the team know that you'll be setting up one-on-one sessions to get to know them better and that you'll be setting up a more formal meeting at a later date.

You may wonder why meeting your team sooner rather than later is crucial or why you want to meet them but want to avoid making any initial changes. This introductory meeting signifies to the team that they are important and conveys that you will take the time to understand the current way of doing business before coming into the role and making decisions.

CHAPTER 5: HOLD EFFECTIVE MEETINGS

"When leaders know how to lead great meetings, there's less time wasted and less frustration."

Justin Rosenstein

While meetings are necessary for our work, they should be productive, collaborative places where you bring your team together. Oh, those long and boring meetings where nothing of consequence was discussed – we've all been through some of those. There are also meetings that you leave thinking if it was even necessary, and an email would have sufficed to disseminate the information discussed. Despite these bad experiences, meetings have a purpose; believe it or not, you can hold effective and productive meetings when implementing these best practices.

Have a Clear Objective

First, you need to determine the purpose of the meeting, and this will guide you in deciding whether or not this meeting is necessary. Do you need the meeting to develop new ideas, get information, or make decisions? Or is it a mix of all of the above? When you are unclear about what you want to accomplish, you can be sure it won't be achieved. The essential item for a meeting to go well is to have a clear goal and a well-planned agenda.

Invite the Right People

Only invite those necessary for the meeting and have the relevant expertise, knowledge, or decision-making authority. This will help keep it focused and productive. If you have a meeting to discuss production goals, there will be no need to invite personnel from the delivery team unless there is a direct correlation between both teams, which you need to discuss. The idea is that when people who are needed are invited, there will be fruitful discussions, versus when persons who are not necessary for the discussion are present, they may feel bored and unwanted in that space and time.

Don't Be Late

Fix the issues of late attendees by starting the meeting on time. Starting on time will send a clear message to latecomers, and you will build a reputation for being on time. People who are late can waste 5 to 10 minutes, if not more, of the meeting time or, in many cases, cause the meeting to run long. Team members who show up on time shouldn't have to wait for those who are always late. Setting a time and keeping it is not only showing employees that company time is valued but also indicating to them that you value their time as well.

Prepare for Follow-up Questions

The worst thing in a meeting is not to answer a simple follow-up question. It's easy to get caught up in making slides for your weekly update deck and not think about how to answer follow-up questions. Be able to explain the "why," "how," and "so what" of the meeting topic.

Set aside time to think of questions the team might ask about the information you've shared.

Prepare answers to those points to be ready if they arise. It doesn't mean you wasted time preparing if a question isn't asked. You've learned more about what you were talking about, which will be helpful in future discussions.

Encourage Participation

Encourage participation from all attendees and create an environment where the team feels comfortable sharing their ideas and opinions. This will help ensure that all perspectives are considered. Remember that this is a team. Value every member and let them know that their opinion matters. But as the leader, you will be the one to determine which ideas are best to implement.

Continuously Evaluate and Improve

Now that the meeting is over, now what? Effective leaders should not just move on to the next task. After each meeting, evaluate its effectiveness and identify areas for improvement for future meetings. This will help you continually improve your meetings' quality and productivity.

Avoid Multitasking at All Costs

One of the worst things you can do in a meeting is to try to do more than one thing at once. Typing annoys your team and makes it harder for them to pay attention to what is being said. You're more likely to miss a question meant for you or look like you don't care about what other people have to say. If necessary, record the meetings if you need to make extensive notes on what is being said. Avoid answering emails. Unless essential for the meeting, cultivate a policy to silence all electronics.

CHAPTER 6: LEAD THROUGH COMMUNICATION

"How well we communicate is not determined by how well we say things but how well we are understood."

Andrew Grove

Communicating as a great leader refers to one's ability to effectively transmit and receive messages with others at all levels. A leader must convey information in a way that is understandable to everyone. It is an additional responsibility and a skill that every successful leader must attain to succeed. Verbal communication is the most recognized tool a leader uses to invoke, inspire, motivate, provide feedback, and report to others. A leader can also use communication to improve the overall efficiency of their teams and enhance their productivity. But also remember that nonverbal communication does impact team goals. How you act as a leader is as important as what you say. Ensure that your actions match your words.

I can remember a time when I was working with a client, and he shared that as a new leader, he was asked into the vice president's office and told that many of his staff had provided negative feedback. My client could not determine why all the feedback was regarding his communication. After working with the client and obtaining a little more information, I learned that he was communicating with the team the way he wanted to be communicated to. I recommended that to improve his communication, he should utilize several communication styles to meet each team member's communication needs. After varying his communication technique, his 360-degree evaluation greatly improved.

What are some of the communication styles he used, and how was he able to tailor such to meet the needs of team members? A more detailed view of effective communication as leaders, as discussed below, will provide insight into the qualities that help leaders be more effective communicators.

Qualities of Effective Leadership Communication

Leaders must learn and adapt these essential qualities of good communication. Some of these qualities include:

- **Clarity**
  One of the most critical aspects of effective communication is that every leader needs to learn and adapt. A leader needs to convey a clear message; otherwise, those working under him will become confused. This confusion will give rise to conflicts and misunderstandings. In other words, if a leader cannot communicate clearly, he won't be able to lead successfully. This is why the words spoken by a leader should be clear to their audience. The goal of clarity is to ensure there are little to no misunderstandings. This quality of communication can be acquired through practice and communication exercises.

- **Empathy**
  When a leader shows empathy towards his followers while communicating, they will be

better able to connect with them. This deeper connection helps leaders forge better bonds and inspire people on a much deeper level. Ultimately, it benefits the whole organization because the workforce will be more motivated and inspired.

- **Confidence**
  Leaders should exude confidence and also must inspire confidence in others through their actions and words. This is only possible if the leader has confidence and can communicate with the followers in a confident yet inspiring tone. Note here that confidence does not mean arrogance.

- **Flexibility**
  When communicating as a leader, you must be as flexible as possible. Flexibility is crucial and allows leaders to adapt their style while communicating. It is essential because it helps leaders deal with changing situations and different team members more effectively.

- **Transparency**
  Transparency boosts a culture of trust and honesty, which in the long run, helps leaders earn the respect of their colleagues and

followers. A leader also needs to communicate with the audience with more openness. This does not mean that the team should always be privy to discussions amongst other team members, as there should be some level of confidentiality. However, transparency ensures that team members are clearly aware of expectations and provided with needed feedback. They should also be allowed to ask questions and openly share their feedback with you.

Effective Communication Strategies

While understanding the qualities of effective communication is needed, new leaders may need additional assistance in how to effectively apply them. Below are some strategies to help leaders improve their communication skills.

- **Practice Active Listening.**
  Communication skills combine listening, speaking, and non-verbal communication. Anyone who wants to be an effective communicator must practice active listening. Active listening goes beyond just hearing the words being said; it also seeks to truly understand the meaning of what is being said and the intent of the message.

As you listen, be truly present in the conversation and make eye contact. You are not listening so that you can prepare a rebuttal, but you are observing nonverbal cues and asking open-ended questions to elicit further responses so that there is no misunderstanding.

- **Develop Emotional Intelligence.**
  Yes, this term has come up again. Now you see how valuable emotional intelligence is to your role as a leader. So, developing emotional intelligence is also an important strategy to help leaders become better communicators. Emotional intelligence enables you to understand the context more efficiently and helps you empathize with others. It allows you to build emotional connections or bonds with others that can be later utilized to inspire them.

- **Practice Public Speaking.**
  It is also one of the vital strategies that can help anyone improve their overall communication potential. Public speaking at different events, places, and meetings helps reduce stage fright. Speaking in

public also enables you to become more aware of your audience and improve your communication. A live audience provides you with feedback that you can use to enhance your communication style further. Even introverted leaders can be great public speakers if they practice this skill.

- **Improve Nonverbal Communication.** Nonverbal communication includes many things, from dressing to body movements of the speaker and hand gestures. Nonverbal communication is also significant for leaders who want to communicate more efficiently. To improve your nonverbal communication, you should watch other influential leaders while they are talking or presenting. Notice their movements, gestures, and demeanor. How did this impact their message? Were you more inspired by these cues, or did you find them distracting you from the message? Use your interpretation of their nonverbal communication to improve your nonverbal communication with others.

- **Familiarize Yourself with Current Communication Technologies.**

  The style of communication and communication technologies are rapidly changing. The world has come a long way from letter writing and printed reports. Leaders must embrace current methods of communication. For example, writing effective emails, conducting video conferences, and attending team meetings online. Learning about effective current technologies and how to use them correctly can provide leaders with extra leverage while communicating as a leader.

As you can see, leaders need to be good communicators, as it is a critical requirement for being a successful leader in almost every field. Leaders must take the stage whenever required to inspire and motivate those working with them. Ensuring that you embody these crucial qualities and implement the strategies provided while communicating will help anyone who wants to become a better leader and will help them communicate as a leader.

CHAPTER 7: BE A VISIBLE LEADER

"As the leader, part of the job is to be visible and willing to communicate with everyone."

Bill Walsh

A visible leader is someone who is present and approachable and represents active communication. This individual also demonstrates core leadership values while energetically and enthusiastically supporting their team. The term visible leader encompasses more than leaders in high positions but includes everyone who leads a team working for a shared goal. Being present, approachable, and willing to take a stand whenever needed are some of the key qualities of visible leaders that differentiate them from those who are absent in mind and body from the team. A visible leader inspires through actions and motivates others to be exceptional.

A visible leader's presence uplifts morale and makes everyone believe their goals are achievable. The presence of a visible leader is significant to any organization's success. When visible, leaders build trust, rapport, and a sense of community and provide a shared objective for everyone. Not only that, but visible leadership also helps create a safe, positive work culture for everyone involved. It also helps in driving innovation and creating a growth-focused environment.

Benefits Of Being a Visible Leader

Being more visible helps not only the leader in achieving their team's goals but also the organization in achieving success. A few of the key benefits of being a visible leader are:

- **Builds Trust and Credibility**
  Being more visible helps you establish trust and credibility among your senior leadership, peers, and team. A leader who is available to the team builds stronger relationships with them. This leads to building trust and credibility. Team members show better confidence

when they know their leader listens to their ideas, provides backup if needed, and supports them. In other words, a team thrives if they know their leader has their back. This creates a healthy relationship between a leader and their team based on trust and credibility.

- **Increases Employee Engagement**
  A visible leader inspires people around him to be more proactive, which helps generate better employee engagement. When leaders regularly communicate with their team, the team is more likely to listen to them, sometimes more than other company communication, which boosts team engagement.

- **Improves Communication**
  A visible leader develops an environment that encourages the team to communicate and improves overall communication within an organization, helping create a healthy flow of ideas and reducing the risk of misunderstanding or errors. Remember that as a leader, you should be a living example. Communicate in a manner that you wish to be

communicated with, and the team will follow suit.

- **Fosters Innovation and Strong Decision-Making**
  The presence of a visible and approachable leader fosters an innovative environment. It also provides a basis for solid decision-making. A visible leader creates a culture of sharing information and new ideas. The team is encouraged to use the information obtained and make sound decisions based on the available information.

- **Develops Leadership Skills**
  Being more visible also helps develop better leadership skills. When leaders are visible, they get better feedback on each of their decisions, which allows them to learn from their mistakes, evolve, and make better decisions in the future. Being a leader does not mean that you already know everything. Your leadership role is an ever-revolving cycle, and you should aim to be a lifelong learner and always aim to improve in all areas of your leadership.

How To Become a Visible Leader?

To become a more visible leader, you can follow these five steps:

1. **Connect With Team Members**
   Connecting with your team members makes you more present and engaged, making you more visible.

2. **Be Accessible**
   If a leader wants to be more visible, they must be more accessible and approachable. Being accessible cultivates a culture that allows the team to know they can come to you when they are burdened with a problem or to make a suggestion.

3. **Share Your Vision**
   Leaders must be able to share their vision to ensure understanding and help the team in achieving that vision.

4. **Take A Stand When Necessary**
   A visible leader must take a stand and make decisions. While no one likes a decision not made in their favor, it is equally true that people do not like

working for indecisive leaders. A visible leader can make tough decisions or take a minority stance.

5. **Lead by Example**
   Visible leaders lead by doing and are an example for their team. That is why anyone who wants to be a more visible leader must also learn the art of leading by example.

By developing a clear vision, building strong relationships, communicating effectively, leading by example, and being proactive, one can become a leader who inspires, motivates, and empowers their team to achieve their best. Becoming a visible leader is an ongoing process that requires dedication, commitment, and hard work. However, the rewards of being a visible leader are significant, including increased trust and respect from your team, improved performance, and a more positive workplace culture. That is why every leader should strive to be visible at all times within their organization.

CHAPTER 8: RELATIONSHIPS MATTER

"Almost everything in leadership comes back to relationships."

Mike Krzyzewski

Leadership is often defined by a person's ability to guide and inspire others toward achieving a common goal. However, successful leadership is much more than that. Based on what you have read so far, you have already deciphered that successful leaders understand the importance of building relationships and creating connections with the people they lead.

The Importance of Building Relationships in Leadership

Building relationships is a critical aspect of effective leadership for several reasons. Some of these have already been discussed so far but are reiterated for emphasis.

- **Trust**
  Building relationships is a crucial component of developing trust. When leaders take the time to get to know their team members, they can better understand their strengths, weaknesses, and motivations. This understanding helps leaders build trust with their team, which is essential for success. I know it's been a while since we spoke about Margaret's experience, but let's look at that here. Consider that she did try to get to know her team members through the introductions, but was that enough? She should have taken some time to get to know the team and build trust before starting to discuss her expectations. How would the team effectively work to meet the goals she has set without gaining some level of trust in her leadership skills? I know I would follow a leader who I am confident has not only the company's best

interest at heart but also the team's.

- **Communication**
  Effective communication is a cornerstone of successful leadership, and building relationships is critical to creating open lines of communication. When leaders take the time to build relationships with their team, they can communicate more effectively, reducing misunderstandings and improving overall productivity.

- **Engagement**
  Engagement is critical in creating a successful team, and building relationships are essential to fostering engagement. When team members feel their leader cares about them and their success, they are more likely to be engaged and motivated to work towards common goals.

Building Relationships: Key Strategies

Building relationships requires a deliberate effort on the part of any leader, especially a new leader. Here are vital strategies for building relationships with your team:

- **Show Genuine Interest**
  Emotional Intelligence! You might have seen this word so many times in this book so far. To build relationships, leaders must show genuine interest in each team member. Trust me...the team members will know if you are being disingenuous. This can involve taking the time to learn about their interests, goals, and concerns. Leaders can show interest by asking open-ended questions, listening actively, and following up on conversations.

- **Practice Empathy**
  Empathy is a critical skill for building relationships. Empathy involves listening, acknowledging feelings, and being understanding. Empathetic leaders can better understand the perspective of their team members and can tailor their communication and leadership styles to meet their needs better.

- **Communicate Effectively**
  Again, effective communication is essential for building relationships. Leaders should communicate regularly with their team, providing feedback,

setting expectations, and ensuring everyone is on the same page. Leaders should also be open to feedback and willing to listen to the concerns and ideas of their team.

- **Be Transparent**
  Transparency is essential for building trust and fostering open communication. Leaders should be transparent about their goals, priorities, and decision-making processes. By being transparent, leaders can help their team members understand the reasoning behind decisions and feel more engaged.

- **Celebrate Successes**
  Celebrating successes is a critical aspect of building relationships. Celebrating success helps build morale and fosters a sense of teamwork and camaraderie. Leaders should take the time to recognize and celebrate their team's achievements, whether big or small. There can also be rewards such as bonuses, promotions, or raises. But sometimes, simply telling someone "good job" and even offering a small certificate or plaque can boost team

morale more than you can ever think.

Being a good and effective leader is about more than just guiding and inspiring a team toward a common goal. Successful leaders understand the importance of building relationships with their team members and fostering trust, communication, and engagement. By practicing strategies such as showing genuine interest, practicing empathy, communicating effectively, being transparent, and celebrating successes, leaders can build strong relationships with their team members, leading to incredible success and achievement for everyone involved.

CHAPTER 9: MANAGING DIFFICULT TEAM MEMBERS

"Dealing with employee issues can be difficult, but not dealing with them can be worse."

Paul Foster

Let's be honest; being a new leader will not be a bed of roses. There is no guarantee that what you have been taught so far in this book will result in a team without challenges. You will, more often than not, encounter difficult team members. Difficult team members can hurt productivity and make being part of the team unpleasant. Leaders must be able to deal with difficult employees, talk with them about their behavior and performance issues, and make a clear plan to address any concerns. If the employee's performance does not improve with feedback and help, you may have to take action to terminate the employee for the sake of the business and the morale of the team.

Tips to Improve Performance

The tips below provide actions that assist in improving workplace performance.

Critique Behavior, Not People

Be objective. Avoid becoming too personal or emotional in the conversation. It's essential to focus on the employee's bad or wrong behavior instead of attacking them as a person. Remember that bad behavior can be caused by confusion, fear, or personal problems that you may be unaware of. The goal is to solve the problem, not to start a fight.

Listen to Feedback

Have a two-way conversation about the issue. Be an active listener! Listen to what the employee says so you can figure out the cause of the behavior and address it. Sometimes, just making the employees feel like they are being heard is enough to make them feel better and change their behavior.

Give Clear Feedback

Managers sometimes have difficulty giving negative feedback, but it's essential to provide clear examples of the bad behavior and explain why it's wrong and how it needs to change. Focusing on specific examples can help the employee feel less defensive and give them helpful information that can help them do a better job at work.

Document Problematic Behavior

When you see poor performance or behavior that worries you, write it down in detail and include the date. Proper documentation helps you remember and talk about specific events and protects the organization if the employee is let go and decides to sue for wrongful termination.

Work Together Toward a Solution

When you talk to a problematic employee about their behavior, the best action is to work together to find a solution you both agree upon. Talk about both the bad and correct behavior, and then find out what the employee needs from you to improve.

Write Down Expectations

Develop a clear plan of action that includes a timeline and a way to evaluate success. Describe the performance that needs to change and how long it will take to complete the performance modification. Sign the plan and have the employee sign it, too. Both of you should keep a copy of the document so that the employee can use it to carry out the plan, and you can use it to measure performance in the future.

Set Specific Consequences

The improvement plan might fail if you don't set clear consequences for the employee's behavior modification in the agreed-upon timeline. Some possible consequences are a formal written warning, being unable to get promotions or bonuses, and, worst-case scenario, being fired.

Monitor Progress

Give your team members as much time as they need to change within reason. During that time, keep track of their progress and any problems or setbacks. Remember to check in as often as you need to monitor their process, stepping in if the employee gets off track. Schedule an in-person evaluation to discuss how the situation has changed after the improvement plan deadline.

Dealing with difficult team members is challenging. While you do not want to allow them to bring the whole team down, you do want to provide time for the team member to correct their behavior. However, there may be instances where removing the person from the team is the only option.

.

CHAPTER 10: DELEGATE, DELEGATE, DELEGATE

"Deciding what not to do is as important as deciding what to do."

Jessica Jackley

As a leader, you will likely always have responsibility for more things than you can handle by yourself. It's unreasonable to think you can successfully plan and perform every task. If you believe your team is not ready to take on tasks alone and you never delegate, they will never be prepared.

Added to this already fragile dilemma, we have a new leader who may not be confident and sure of their role or may have a preconceived notion that there is only one right way of doing anything.

Learning the art of delegation is a significant skill that can lead to your success.

Delegation is giving control, authority, or responsibility to another person. For leaders, delegation is essential to best use time and resources. It also provides your team members with delegated tasks an opportunity to develop and grow.

Now that you understand the importance of delegation, let's talk about how to delegate successfully. Have you ever looked at the final product of a task you had assigned somebody else and realized you didn't get what you wanted and would have to redo it yourself? Initially, you probably thought that the person given the task failed, but that's often not true. As we further discuss delegation, you may realize you, as the delegator, failed.

Importance of Delegating Tasks

Many may think leaders delegate simply because they want to avoid performing specific tasks. This is not true! A leader cannot and should not do all tasks. Learning the skill of delegation empowers your team, helps build trust, and allows you to develop others. Delegation enables you to identify individuals within your team with valuable skills that can be further developed for the betterment of the team. Taking on more responsibility as a leader is only possible with effective delegation that's empowering, motivating, and encourages greater responsibility and accountability among team members.

Developing your Delegation Skills

You and your employees need to be productive and valuable. A successful leader develops others and strives to help them reach their full potential. Currently, most people work at 50 percent of their capacity. Tapping into that unused 50-percent potential through effective delegation can significantly increase productivity.

Three Steps of Delegation

For many, delegation can be a daunting task. However, there are only three steps to delegation.

1. Delegation begins with thinking through the task that needs to be done. Clearly define your objectives and the desired outcome.

2. Setting performance standards is the second step in delegation. In what ways will you measure the quality of the work completed?

3. In the third step, you must set a deadline and, in some instances, a timeline for getting the work done. For critical tasks or those with a more extended deadline, milestones should be added, or a timeline should be identified.

Elements of Effective Delegation

Now that you've been provided with the three steps to delegating, additional elements go into managing and delegating effectively.

1. **Identify the Right Person**
   The wrong person being selected for a critical task is one of the main reasons for delegation failure.

2. **Make the Perfect Match**
   A well-informed match between the job's requirements and a person's abilities is imperative. When assigning someone a task, make sure they are qualified to do

the job.

3. **Provide Confidence**
   Develop the confidence and competence of staff by delegating smaller tasks first before easing into larger, more complex tasks.

4. **Clarify Goals**
   Be crystal clear about the expected outcome and set clear expectations. Whenever possible, provide examples or any processes that must be followed. Explain what you need, identify available resources, and provide relevant information. Setting clear, realistic, and measurable goals is essential to delegation.

5. **Empower the Delegate**
   Only when the appropriate authority is provided to the delegated team member will optimal results be achieved.

6. **Ensure Appropriate Resources are Available**
   To those completing delegated tasks, available time and money must be identified, as well as whom they should

turn to for assistance and to ask questions.

7. **Give Credit**
   Provide recognition of those who completed the delegated task. Providing credit will create a more engaged team and fuel the team's potential to rise to higher achievement.

Through delegation, and by including these elements in your delegation process, you can develop your team to take on larger and more complex tasks with great success.

CHAPTER 11: MOTIVATING YOUR TEAM

"To build a strong team, you must see someone else's strength as a complement to your weakness and not a threat to your position or authority."

Christine Craine

While motivation is often mercurial, there is no doubt that motivation plays an essential role in any organization. Motivated employees are vital to an organization and are often among its greatest assets. Further, motivated employees directly contribute to an organization's success. Therefore, as a new leader, you must understand the power of employee motivation.

What is Employee Motivation?

Motivation is a behavior, and an environment should be created to provide employees with optimal motivation. That sounds easier than it is. Employee motivation is tangible and intangible and focuses on how engaged an employee feels in correlation to an organization's goals and results. Employee motivation is determined by the enthusiasm, energy level, commitment, and creativity demonstrated daily in the workplace.

Motivation falls into two categories - intrinsic and extrinsic. Intrinsic motivation comes from within, by their belief system or desire to do well. An employee's beliefs are usually innate and are considered one of the most embedded motivational factors. Employees with deep-rooted beliefs often desire success, and their motivation can be increased through praise and positive feedback. Extrinsic motivation is based on external factors, such as awards, rewards, and recognition. Getting a raise in pay or a promotion are examples of extrinsic motivation and surely in a great factor in improving staff performance. External stimulation can also promote employee willingness to learn new skills and improve intrinsic motivation.

10 Ways to Motivate Employees

Here are a few simple ways to motivate your employees in the workplace.

1. **Recognize good work.**
   An employer-employee relationship is strengthened when recognition is provided.

2. **Provide intrinsic rewards.**
   Motivate your employees from within. Extrinsic rewards fade quickly.

3. **Provide autonomy, not bureaucracy.**
   Micromanagement is a mistake. Don't dictate. When hiring employees with the proper skill set, you should serve more as a facilitator.

4. **Offer a good environment.**
   Motivate your staff by creating an amazing work environment.

5. **Support employee well-being.**
   While incentives are a great motivator, employees cannot provide their best work if they are unwell, tired, or overwhelmed. Addressing your employees' mental, emotional, and physical health is an

excellent way of keeping them performing at their peak.

6. **Lead with vision.**
   Employees must be motivated and know their efforts are making a difference. To reach their destination, they must know where to go and, more importantly, how to get there.

7. **Explain why.**
   Ensure each team member knows their role in achieving the company's mission. When everyone knows how their actions fit with the rest of the picture, it can provide additional motivation.

8. **Seek employee feedback.**
   Solicit employee feedback, suggestions, and ideas. Once received, ensure that their feedback, suggestions, ideas, and grievances are reviewed and addressed within a reasonable time.

9. **Develop career paths.**
   Work with each team member and develop a clear and transparent career plan that specifies their roles and

responsibilities and how to get from one level to the next.

10. **Maintain flexibility.**
    Not every team member has the exact needs. To motivate and keep your team happy, you should allow flexibility.

Motivation ensures that your team remains active and contributes their best. High motivation leads to higher productivity, increased innovation, reduced absenteeism, and lower turnover.

CHAPTER 12: LEADING VIRTUALLY

"Remember to enjoy the freedom of being able to work from anywhere and the flexibility to adapt your work to your life rather than the other way around."

Alex Muench

Leadership is about making others better due to your presence and ensuring that impact lasts in your absence. It exists even when people are not in front of you. Leadership is about being available to guide and help others. Even before the COVID-19 pandemic, there were leaders who operated remotely. During the pandemic, this number significantly increased, and the skills of leading virtually became most important to be further developed. This shift did not negatively impact their leadership skills as they adopted and used technology to positively impact productivity and remain visible in the virtual workspace. So, note that leading virtually requires the use of technology effectively to support their remote team. Leaders who do this well have more engaged, higher-performing employees.

Establishing ground rules and identifying the collaboration tools are two considerations that must be addressed when leading virtually. Collaboration tools allow the team to communicate more efficiently. The tools selected vary from organization to organization. Ground rules can be provided to the team, or as a team, you can decide the rules and expectations together to get the most buy-in and efficiency for the virtual interactions. These rules could include how often people will be expected to contact each other, whether the team will use chat or direct messages, the expected response time for communication, etc. Collaboration tools, for which there are many, can make group interactions more efficient.

When leading virtually:

Be transparent. Get employees updated about

what's going on with projects. This helps them stay current and feel more comfortable communicating with you when they need help or have questions.

Lead by example. Actions always speak louder than words. If you expect people to contact you for help or take the initiative, ensure you are available.

Use technology well. Technology allows leaders to communicate across time zones easily, but it can also be inefficient if not used correctly. Establishing which forms of communication will be used for what purposes reduces confusion about when something should be done or answered via chat versus email.

Focus on quality, not speed. All communication should be reviewed before sending. Considering your responses carefully is much more important than answering immediately, as miscommunication may occur due to different time zones or cultures/languages being used.

Provide context. Ensure people know what's happening outside their team so they aren't left in the dark when they need information. This could be through group chat, updating projects in software tools, or other means to avoid anyone being stuck not knowing what's going on outside of their part of the work.

There are other considerations as a leader that you should make your team aware of as well, such as when working virtually:

Be proactive. There are fewer boundaries to make us feel like we can't send a message about something that doesn't belong specifically to our role. This benefits people who may not always ask questions because they don't want to bother others or feel they shouldn't speak up if it isn't relevant to them. If you see an opportunity for your team to do something better but don't say anything, you're not prioritizing them or identifying ways to improve.

Be considerate. When sending emails, use clear and concise language and respond promptly. If you don't get back to someone immediately, provide regular updates if they are waiting for your information.

Be available. When working virtually, check in often with your team. Keep in contact, even if it's to say hello. This shows that you value them and genuinely want to know how things are going for them.

Be supportive. When people aren't face-to-face, less body language is available to help determine what the person means when communicating. Therefore, a supportive tone is essential to ensure people know you're listening and understand what they say.

CONCLUSION

"Innovation distinguishes between a leader and a follower.

Steve Jobs

Now that you have reached the end of the book consider looking back at the scenario of Margaret as shared in the Introduction. What approach will you take with all that has been discussed related to how one can be effective in your new leadership role? Think about setting your expectations early. Should this be something that you discuss at length in the first meeting with your team? Note that you need to truly understand your role and get to know those whom you are leading before you set out a clear plan of goals and expectations. Also, remember that goals are revolving, so these will have to be revisited from time to time. The essence here is not to be like Margaret. Though you will make mistakes as a new leader, use the tips provided in this book to plan ahead.

So, remember that you need to set your expectations early and continue to develop a positive leadership attitude. As you do so, you will need to truly embody the qualities of a good leader before attending your first meeting. Remember that this first meeting is about getting to know your team so that you can put a game plan in place that will be best for the strengths and weaknesses of your team. You are not leading for leading sake; you are leading your team to win! Then continue to hold effective meetings - ones that have a clear purpose and will be most beneficial to the success of the team. Therefore, it is important to remember the need for good communication skills. Communicating your goals and expectations with your team and being an active listener is necessary. The final reminders are to be a visible leader and focus on building relationships, even with difficult team members, as these matter to a team's success.

Now being equipped with the needed knowledge

and strategies, it is time to take on your new role with the confidence of an effective leader. I'm a leader; now what? Go and make your team a success.

ABOUT THE AUTHOR

Dr. Wendy Norfleet is a renowned leader and entrepreneur recognized for her outstanding achievements. She currently serves as the Chief Executive Officer for Norfleet Integrated Solutions, a premier organization that provides strategic and innovative solutions for businesses to scale and enhance their leadership capabilities. Dr. Norfleet's strengths lie in her extensive leadership experience, comprehensive business knowledge, unwavering determination, exceptional creativity, and strong IT background. She is highly motivated to overcome challenges, particularly those that benefit her clients.

Dr. Norfleet is also a respected leader in her community, having received numerous awards for her achievements. She was recently named as a 2023 Top Entrepreneur, 2021 Small Business Leader of the Year, and 2020 Woman of Influence, and presented with the 2021 Corporate Vision Award for Best Business Consulting and Coaching Company in North Florida.

Dr. Norfleet is an active member of the community and loves to mentor and work with those aspiring to be great leaders.

www.ingramcontent.com/pod-product-compliance
Lightning Source LLC
LaVergne TN
LVHW050609100826
845148LV00015B/3187